Appalachian Regional Commission

The Appalachian Regional Commission (ARC) is a regional economic development agency representing a unique partnership of federal, state, and local government. Established by an act of Congress in 1965, the Commission is composed of the governors of the 13 Appalachian states and a federal co-chair, who is appointed by the president. Local participation is provided through multi-county local development districts with boards made up of elected officials, businesspeople, and other local leaders. Each year Congress appropriates funds for Commission programs, which ARC allocates among its member states. The governors draw up annual state Appalachian strategies and select projects for approval by the federal co-chair. ARC projects include a safe and efficient highway system; education, job-training, and health-care programs; water and sewer systems; and other essentials of comprehensive economic development.

Appalachia

Appalachia, as defined in the legislation from which the Appalachian Regional Commission derives its authority, is a 205,000-square-mile region that follows the spine of the Appalachian Mountains from southern New York to northern Mississippi. The Appalachian Region includes all of West Virginia and parts of 12 other states: Alabama, Georgia, Kentucky, Maryland, Mississippi, New York, North Carolina, Ohio, Pennsylvania, South Carolina, Tennessee, and Virginia.

Contents

Preface

The Appalachian Regional Commission has a key role in helping the people of Appalachia build a better future: creating jobs, building infrastructure to foster business and community growth and to connect the Region with national and international markets, and developing an educated, healthy workforce prepared to participate fully in the global economy.

Appalachia has made significant progress in addressing its historical challenges, but ARC's vision for the Region has not yet been achieved. In fiscal year 2010, more than 80 counties were still classified as economically distressed. Increased global competition and technological change have resulted in job losses and restructuring in many key Appalachian industries. Because of its rugged terrain and high proportion of rural residents, Appalachia is at risk of falling behind in the implementation and use of modern technology and telecommunications, necessary components of competitiveness in today's economy.

In this time of economic challenges and rapid change in the way business is conducted worldwide, ARC is working to ensure that Appalachia's leaders and citizens have the capacity, capability, and resources they need to build and strengthen their local economies. The Commission's structure as a federal-state-local partnership and as a regional agency makes it uniquely suited to help guide and foster the local efforts required for change.

This strategic plan is a guide for ARC to take targeted and measurable action toward its vision of bringing Appalachia into full economic parity with the nation. It outlines goals and objectives that provide clear guidance for priorities and a basis for annual evaluation. It calls for alignment of resources to maximize results and for performance measurement that ensures that the ARC partnership is effective and accountable. It creates a framework for building on past accomplishments to help move Appalachia forward.

Highlights

ARC's Vision for Appalachia
Appalachia will achieve socioeconomic parity with the nation.

ARC's Mission
ARC's mission is to be a strategic partner and advocate for sustainable community and economic development in Appalachia.

General Goals

1: Increase job opportunities and per capita income in Appalachia to reach parity with the nation.
2: Strengthen the capacity of the people of Appalachia to compete in the global economy.
3: Develop and improve Appalachia's infrastructure to make the Region economically competitive.
4: Build the Appalachian Development Highway System to reduce Appalachia's isolation.

Six-Year Performance Goals
Assuming ARC's annual funding remains at the current level, the Commission is committed to the following six-year performance goals:

- 120,000 jobs will be created or retained.
- 120,000 households will be served with new or improved water and sewer infrastructure.
- 120,000 citizens of the Region will benefit from enhanced education and job-related skills.
- 150 miles of the Appalachian Development Highway System will be opened to traffic (based on the current level of transportation funding from the U.S. Congress).

In 1965, Congress established the Appalachian Regional Commission (ARC) to address the profound economic and social problems in the Appalachian Region that made it a "region apart" from the rest of the nation. The Appalachian Regional Development Act established a mandate to focus attention and resources on reducing the socioeconomic gap between the Appalachian Region and the nation through a variety of activities, including advocacy, regional planning, research, and grant making.

The Commission's 2008 reauthorization extends ARC's nonhighway programs through fiscal year (FY) 2012 and continues the Commission's work in providing basic infrastructure and health care, and developing local leadership. It also creates a new energy and economic development initiative; adds ten counties to the Appalachian Region; requires the designation of at-risk counties; and permits ARC to fund projects in economically at-risk counties at up to 70 percent of project costs.

The Appalachian Regional Commission's unique structure is designed to ensure an active federal-state-local partnership. There are 14 Commission members: the governors of the 13 Appalachian states and a federal co-chair. Each year the 13 governors elect one of their peers to serve as the states' co-chair of the Commission. The federal co-chair has one vote and the 13 governors share one vote on Commission decisions. All program strategies, allocations, and other policy matters must be approved by both a majority of the governors and the federal co-chair. This consensus model ensures close collaboration between the federal and state partners in carrying out ARC's mission. Local participation is provided through multi-county local development districts, with boards made up of elected officials, businesspeople, and other local leaders.

Because of its partnership approach, ARC is able to identify and help fund innovative grassroots initiatives that might otherwise languish. In many cases, ARC functions as a predevelopment agency, providing modest initial project funding that is unavailable from other sources. This modest investment leverages other funds, particularly private funds.

Unlike economic development agencies that are primarily categorical grant makers, the Commission performs advocacy, regional planning, and research activities in combination with its special grant programs. No other entity has this regional mandate for Appalachia.

ARC serves as an advocate for the Region by forming partnerships with nonprofits and other agencies; convening regional and subregional forums; identifying regional initiatives and grant priorities for ARC funding support; setting policies that guide investment of flexible ARC funds; and participating in the work of the Interagency Coordinating Council on Appalachia, which is chaired by the ARC federal co-chair.

Research and regional planning activities include developing a knowledge base of problems and opportunities that supports the work of regional leaders; examining the effectiveness of alternate approaches; supporting strategic planning activities in the Appalachian states; and partaking in public policy development that benefits the Region.

These unique planning and advocacy activities vastly multiply the influence and shape of ARC's grant programs.

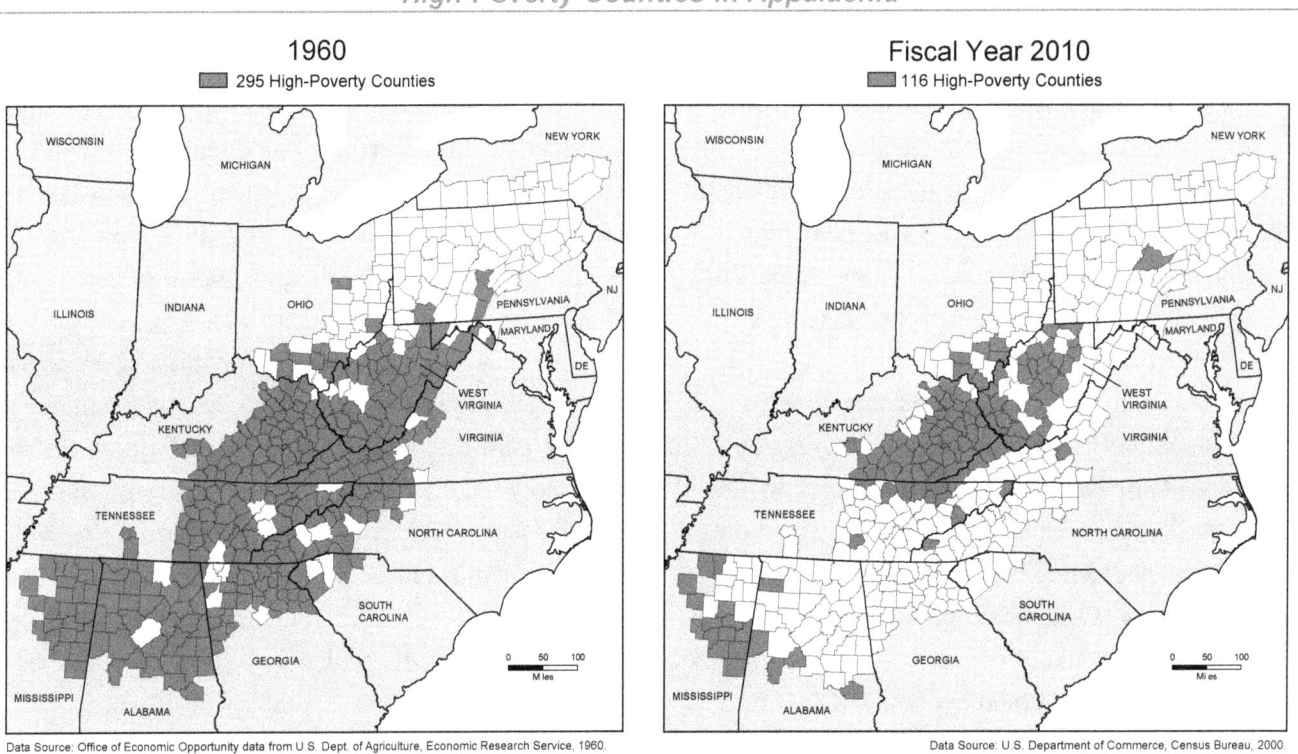

High-Poverty Counties in Appalachia

1960
295 High-Poverty Counties

Data Source: Office of Economic Opportunity data from U.S. Dept. of Agriculture, Economic Research Service, 1960.

Fiscal Year 2010
116 High-Poverty Counties

Data Source: U.S. Department of Commerce, Census Bureau, 2000.

Accomplishments and Challenges

In the mid 1960s, one in three Appalachians lived in poverty and per capita income was 23 percent lower than the U.S. average. In the previous decade nearly 2 million more people had left the Region than had moved into it. Since then, the Appalachian Region has experienced broad socioeconomic improvements, the result of many macroeconomic and social factors, including ARC's activities. For example, the Commission's efforts have helped:

* Reduce the number of high-poverty counties from 295 to 116;
* Create or retain over 7 million jobs;
* Construct over 2,500 miles of new highways;
* Develop over 400 rural health centers;
* Provide water and sewer services to over 900,000 households; and
* Double the percentage of adults with a high school education.

Although Appalachia has seen clear and substantial progress since the early days of the Commission's work, the majority of the Region's communities still do not enjoy the same economic vitality and living conditions that the rest of the country does. The Region continues to battle economic distress, concentrated areas of poverty, high unemployment rates, educational disparities, high rates of disease, and population outmigration.

Development of a New Strategic Plan

ARC updates its strategic plan every six years. The Commission's 2005–2010 strategic plan provided the foundation for the 2011–2016 strategic plan. Through FY 2009, the 2005–2010 strategic plan guided the Commission in adding or retaining 130,000 jobs for Appalachian workers, opening 107 miles of Appalachian highways to traffic, providing new or improved water and sewer systems for 120,000 Appalachian households, and providing training and educational opportunities for 110,000 Appalachian citizens.

The process for developing the new strategic plan involved six steps: (1) holding field forums to obtain citizen input; (2) conducting research, consultations, and a socioeconomic review with an assessment of the Region's economy; (3) hosting a series of online town hall meetings to prioritize regional issues; (4) holding a synthesis session to review the findings of the online town hall meetings, field forums, and research in order to identify issues, opportunities, goals, and strategies; (5) holding a consensus session to review the draft plan and make amendments as needed; and (6) adopting the new strategic plan.

The first step in the planning process involved obtaining citizen input on high-priority regional issues. ARC held five field forums—one each in Pennsylvania, North Carolina, Alabama, Kentucky, and West Virginia. More than 300 citizens participated in the forums, in addition to representatives from ten federal agencies, who participated both to support the ARC planning process and to prepare for a new multi-agency federal Appalachian Regional Development Initiative. Forty-two regional issues were identified in the forums, ranging from job-creation problems to natural-resource opportunities.

ARC then conducted research and consultations on regional issues and opportunities, after which the 42 issues identified in the field forums were presented to regional audiences through a series of online town hall meetings, in which participants were invited to rank each issue. Twenty high-priority issues were identified through this process. (See page 25 for a list of the issues.)

The results of the field forums and online town hall meetings were analyzed, and ARC hosted two working sessions with representatives of the 13 Appalachian states and ARC federal staff to develop the elements of the new strategic plan, reflecting the current issues and concerns of the Region's citizens. The new strategic plan developed during these sessions was adopted by the Commission in November 2010.

This process resulted in a strategic plan that focuses on investments in jobs, infrastructure, education, and training, while considering the need to conserve energy and protect the natural environment.

ARC's Vision for Appalachia

Appalachia will achieve socioeconomic parity with the nation.

ARC's Mission

ARC's mission is to be a strategic partner and advocate for sustainable community and economic development in Appalachia.

General Goals

1. Increase job opportunities and per capita income in Appalachia to reach parity with the nation.
2. Strengthen the capacity of the people of Appalachia to compete in the global economy.
3. Develop and improve Appalachia's infrastructure to make the Region economically competitive.
4. Build the Appalachian Development Highway System to reduce Appalachia's isolation.

See Appendix A for more information on the strategic planning process. See Appendix B for program evaluations and research used in preparing the strategic plan.

Guiding Principles and Regional Development Roles

To meet its mission, ARC will rely on the following guiding principles:

- Promote homegrown solutions.
- Create sustainable economic development.
- Address persistent economic distress.
- Seed innovation.
- Stimulate investments by federal, state, and local agencies; philanthropies; and the private sector.
- Support inclusive local decision making.
- Act as a clearinghouse for ideas and expertise.
- Capitalize on existing assets.
- Encourage lifelong learning.
- Seek regional solutions.
- Strengthen global competitiveness.

These principles underlie ARC's five regional development roles: advocate, knowledge builder, partner, investor, and catalyst.

- **Advocate.** ARC is an advocate for the Region with federal and state agencies, nonprofits, and other organizations. This advocacy produces increased levels of technical assistance, funding, and policy attention.
- **Knowledge Builder.** ARC's knowledge base uniquely positions the agency to provide focus on problems and development opportunities. ARC builds expert knowledge through research, regional forums, advisory councils, and community meetings.
- **Partner.** The ARC development approach is based on a unique federal-state-local government partnership that expedites project development and solves problems that cannot be addressed by one level of government alone.
- **Investor.** ARC creates economic opportunities in the Region by making its funds available for seed capital, gap funding, and investments in innovative programs.

- **Catalyst.** ARC often provides modest project funding that attracts investment from other agencies, nonprofits, and the private sector. The Commission leverages over eight times the amount of its investment by attracting private investment.

ARC's guiding principles and regional development roles provide the necessary framework for successfully implementing the Commission's new strategic plan. This approach underlies ARC's strategy to invest in people; in basic infrastructure, including highways; and in job creation and retention.

Challenges to Implementing the Strategic Plan

ARC can effectively and efficiently implement its FY 2011–2016 strategies and achieve its performance goals, assuming that it obtains sufficient resources to carry out its planned activities. However, several external factors might affect ARC's ability to achieve its goals.

- Economic downturns, which generally hit deeper in the Appalachian Region and last longer, could adversely impact achievement of ARC's performance goals.
- Government regulations and policies could influence ARC efforts to achieve the performance goals.
- ARC is a partnership of 13 states and the federal government that works in concert with 73 local development districts. Budget constraints and policy redirection within the Appalachian states and local development districts can hinder the pursuit of ARC goals.
- Inconsistent or inadequate funding would impact ARC's ability to implement its strategic plan.
- Unanticipated demographic shifts in the Appalachian Region, such as an increase in population aging and high levels of settlement by people with low educational attainment, could affect achievement of ARC's performance goals.

General Goal 1:
Increase Job Opportunities and Per Capita Income in
Appalachia to Reach Parity with the Nation

Changes to the Region's economic base present significant opportunities and challenges to Appalachia. The new economy offers opportunities for the Region in knowledge-based industries and sectors such as services and health care. At the same time, shifting demands present challenges to traditional manufacturing, mining, and agriculture.

In partnership with other agencies, ARC will help local and state leaders diversify local economies, support entrepreneurship, increase domestic and global markets, and foster new technologies in order to address job shifts throughout the Region. In addition, ARC will encourage local leaders to build on the opportunities presented by Appalachian highway corridors and to examine heritage, cultural, and recreational assets that can create job opportunities while preserving the character of the Region's communities.

Strategic Objective 1.1: Develop Leaders and Strengthen Community Capacity

As a community or region seeks to develop a healthy, competitive, and sustainable economy, it needs to build the capacity of three interdependent elements: individual leaders, organizations, and the community as a whole. Leadership-development skills, broad citizen involvement, strategic planning processes, and collaborations among business, government, nonprofit, and philanthropic organizations contribute to a sense of empowerment and sustained economic well-being. These activities foster broad-based civic engagement and support strategic readiness to take advantage of economic opportunities.

Selected Strategies:
- Support the development of broad-based leadership structures and transformative institutions for change,

such as community-development foundations and community-development financial institutions.

- Build the capacity to collaborate among government, business, and nonprofit and philanthropic sectors by improving skills in consensus building, communication, networking, knowledge and understanding of economic and social trends, and other elements of civic capacity.
- Support strategic planning initiatives for local and regional organizations to capitalize on economic development opportunities.
- Encourage partnerships and promote regional efforts in economic development.
- Provide training and consultation services to local governments and nonprofit organizations engaged in economic development.

Strategic Objective 1.2: Diversify the Economic Base

For Appalachia to compete in the global economy, the Region must expand efforts to diversify its economic base to provide new employment opportunities.

Prosperity and stability for Appalachian communities will depend on their ability to find new business and economic opportunities that can build on the Region's strengths while diversifying its base.

Selected Strategies:

- Encourage the establishment and development of workforce training programs, entrepreneurial support, and export activities, and the promotion of technological advances and technology-related businesses and services.
- Expand efforts to modernize and strengthen existing businesses.
- Develop new businesses that can expand the economic foundation of the Region.
- Raise awareness about economic development tools communities can use to strengthen and diversify their economic base.

Strategic Objective 1.3: Enhance Entrepreneurial Activity in the Region

Locally owned businesses play an important role in creating sustainable local economies and improving the quality of life in Appalachian communities, especially in economically distressed areas. Many communities need assistance in developing support for business incubators and providing entrepreneurial training and financial services.

Selected Strategies:

- Improve access to investment capital and credit for local businesses through resources such as venture capital funds, subordinated debt funds, and micro-credit lending programs.
- Educate current and future entrepreneurs through training programs in middle schools, high schools, community colleges, and four-year colleges and universities.
- Nurture local businesses by creating technical assistance networks through business incubators, business associations, and private-sector resources.

Strategic Objective 1.4: Develop and Market Strategic Assets for Local Economies

A recognized way of strengthening communities and their economies is through the identification and development of local cultural, heritage, and natural assets. This approach to development recognizes and builds on indigenous resources, experience, wisdom, skills, and capacity in Appalachian communities.

Creating local homegrown economic opportunity is central to this asset-based approach. Appalachia's arts, crafts, music, and heritage resources and its natural and recreational assets can be leveraged for the economic benefit of the Region.

Selected Strategies:

- Identify local and regional assets for development.
- Create strategies that help existing and new local businesses capitalize on indigenous assets.
- Support efforts to maximize the economic benefits of Appalachian cultural and heritage tourism and crafts industries.

Strategic Objective 1.5: Increase the Domestic and Global Competitiveness of the Existing Economic Base

Many Appalachian communities have embraced not only new domestic business development strategies but also global strategies that promote increased international business activity in order to be competitive. By helping local firms find new markets at home and abroad, communities can assist in job creation. Foreign direct investment is another effective approach that can generate additional job opportunities and help communities enhance their competitive advantage.

Selected Strategies:

- Support research on global and domestic market opportunities.
- Support technical assistance and ongoing business

consultation to help medium and small businesses connect to national and international markets.
- Support foreign direct investment in Appalachia.

Strategic Objective 1.6: Foster the Development and Use of Innovative Technologies

Information technology represents an important opportunity to close the job gap in Appalachia through high-value-added industries such as telecommunications and computing services. Appalachian communities should partner with federal and private-sector research labs, research universities, and other technology organizations to help create and retain technology-related jobs.

Selected Strategies:

- Assist in the creation of telecommunications and computing enterprises.
- Provide assistance for expanding existing high-technology operations in the Region.
- Promote partnerships with, and leverage research opportunities generated by, government-sponsored and private-sector research labs.

- Expand and create technology research initiatives in the Region's colleges and universities.
- Increase support for public-sector science and technology programs.
- Support the commercialization of new technologies developed by federal labs, universities, and other sources.

Strategic Objective 1.7: Capitalize on the Economic Potential of the Appalachian Development Highway System (ADHS)

The ADHS presents perhaps the greatest community and economic development opportunity in the Region. To maximize its potential, programs and activities must be designed to capitalize on the system's connectivity.

Selected Strategies:

- Support local and regional economic and community-development initiatives that effectively use completed sections of the ADHS.
- Encourage strategic planning to help direct and select appropriate development along future segments of the system.
- Promote cooperative projects and programs between economic development officials and highway officials.

Strategic Objective 1.8: Encourage Sustainable Economic Use of Natural Resources

Natural resources such as water, soil, and forests can be used to benefit the economy of the Region. If managed in a sustainable way, these natural resources can provide long-term economic benefit and improved quality of life for local communities.

Selected Strategies:

- Support economically sustainable uses for Appalachia's natural and environmental assets, including its forests and wood products, water features and watersheds, agricultural resources and local food systems, and scenic viewsheds.
- Promote activities and initiatives that effectively use walking, cycling, and other outdoor recreation trails for local economic benefit.
- Encourage research on natural resources that can make a vital contribution to sustainable economic growth in the Appalachian Region.

Strategic Objective 1.9: Encourage Investments in Energy Projects that Create Jobs

Encouraging investments in energy resources in Appalachia can help increase economic opportunities for the Region. By carefully using its energy resources and employing emerging energy technologies and practices, Appalachia can create and retain jobs; increase the supply of locally produced clean, affordable energy; help companies stay competitive; and keep the Region moving toward energy independence.

Selected Strategies:

- Promote energy efficiency in Appalachia to enhance the Region's economic competitiveness.
- Increase the use of renewable energy resources in Appalachia, including wind, solar, geothermal, and biomass, to produce alternative transportation fuels, electricity, and heat.
- Support the development of conventional energy resources in Appalachia, especially advanced clean coal, to produce alternative transportation fuels, electricity, and heat.

General Goal 2:
Strengthen the Capacity of the People of Appalachia to Compete in the Global Economy

In order to compete in the twenty-first-century economy, the people of Appalachia must have the skills and knowledge required to develop, staff, and manage globally competitive businesses. In addition, the Region's communities must provide adequate health care in order to keep existing businesses and develop new ones.

ARC will continue to support local efforts to make all of the Region's citizens productive participants in the global economy. The Commission's focus will be to address a range of educational issues, such as workforce skills, early childhood education, dropout prevention, and improved college attendance; and health issues, such as the recruitment and retention of healthcare professionals in areas with documented shortages and the promotion of better health through wellness and preventive measures. In addition, ARC will develop partnerships with other organizations to

address the disproportionate burden of chronic disease in the Region.

Strategic Objective 2.1: Develop Leaders and Strengthen Community Capacity

Appalachia needs to develop strong leaders, organizations, and communities to promote the Region's competitiveness. Capacity-building activities that strengthen collaborative relationships among communities, agencies, and individuals, that encourage innovative and achievable first steps, and that provide an increase in awareness of, and dialogue on, strategic opportunities contribute to improved community responsibility and use of resources.

Selected Strategies:
- Establish and maintain collaborative relationships between training institutions and businesses to improve workforce readiness.

- Strengthen school-based civic education through service learning and youth community-development efforts.
- Support greater involvement of young people in community activities such as tutoring, peer mediation, and serving on advisory boards.
- Promote community-based dialogue and management of critical local health issues.
- Encourage broad-based, diverse participation in leadership and community capacity building.

Strategic Objective 2.2: Enhance Workforce Skills through Training and Education

As the changing global economy affects Appalachian communities and businesses, many adults in the Region find it difficult to retain their jobs or seek new ones without significant retraining and additional education. Most new jobs are in sectors that require a higher level of education. To respond to new economic opportunities and weather economic uncertainty, workers must continually build skills and experience.

Selected Strategies:
- Support the expansion and modernization of workforce training and education programs in strategic industry sectors.
- Encourage workforce development that supports green jobs in the fields of energy efficiency and conservation, environmental remediation, and alternative energy development.
- Partner with community colleges, technical schools, and universities to support strategic workforce development initiatives.

Strategic Objective 2.3: Increase Access to Quality Child Care and Early Childhood Education

Access to quality child care fosters the development of children and enables their parents and guardians to take advantage of job opportunities. In addition, studies have shown that the benefits of high-quality early childhood education programs, especially for children from low-income families, last at least into early adulthood. Many families in Appalachia often do not have the resources, in terms of finances or time, to take full advantage of such services.

Selected Strategies:
- Support local and regional efforts to increase access to early childhood education programs.
- Promote efforts that increase access to quality child care to support workforce recruitment and retention.

Strategic Objective 2.4: Increase Educational Attainment and Achievement

Research has shown that high levels of educational attainment and achievement are associated with better health for individuals and their children, longer life expectancies, and higher salaries. While progress has been made in improving levels of educational attainment and achievement in Appalachia, resources are still needed to close the gap in educational attainment between the Appalachian Region and the rest of the nation. To strengthen Appalachia's economic competitiveness, more Appalachians need to graduate from

high school and continue with post-secondary education at community colleges, universities, or professional schools.

Selected Strategies:

- Support local and regional efforts to better prepare students, out-of-school youths, and adults for post-secondary-level training.
- Maintain support for and seek expansion of the Appalachian Higher Education Network and other partnerships that increase college-going and college-completion rates.
- Support dropout prevention programs.

Strategic Objective 2.5: Expand Community-Based Wellness and Disease-Prevention Efforts

Appalachia suffers from disproportionately high rates of chronic disease, which has a significant adverse effect on workforce participation and productivity and impedes opportunities for economic development. Community-based wellness and health education efforts are key to reducing health disparities, developing a stronger workforce, and ensuring the long-term vitality of the Appalachian Region.

Selected Strategies:

- Use best practices in public health to develop targeted approaches to wellness and disease prevention.
- Support partnerships that educate children and families about basic health risks and encourage lifelong healthy behaviors.
- Enhance community efforts to improve health-delivery services, especially in communities facing high rates of chronic disease.

Strategic Objective 2.6: Increase the Availability of Affordable, High-Quality Health Care

Many parts of Appalachia, including its most economically distressed counties, are underserved by health-

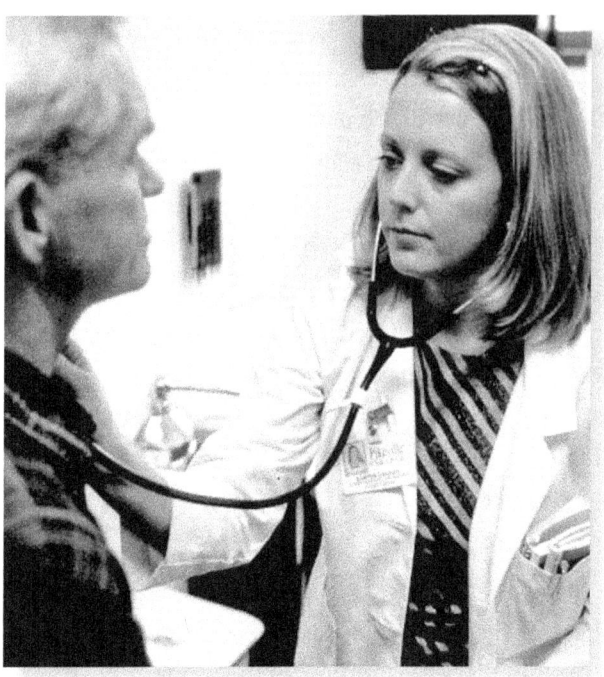

care professionals and health facilities. Activities and policies to improve the supply and distribution of the Region's professional health-care workforce and facilities can help ensure that health care is comprehensive, affordable, and accessible to community residents.

Selected Strategies:

- Expand the Region's supply of quality health-care professionals by attracting new practitioners and offering training and education for members of the health-care workforce.
- Improve facilities and infrastructure to support the provision of high-quality clinical care in underserved areas.
- Use technology to reduce the high cost of health-care services.
- Offer short-term support for sustainable clinical services among underserved populations, especially those in Health Professional Shortage Areas.
- Improve access to health care for under-served populations.

General Goal 3:
Develop and Improve Appalachia's Infrastructure to Make the Region Economically Competitive

In order to compete in the global economy, Appalachia must have the infrastructure necessary for economic development, including water and sewer systems, telecommunications systems, and efficient connections to global transportation networks. But barriers such as rugged terrain and low population density have hindered the Region in developing adequate infrastructure.

ARC will address the lack of adequate water and sewer systems and telecommunications systems and services in the Region, and will build partnerships to address the critical issue of intermodal connections to improve access to the global market.

Strategic Objective 3.1: Develop Leaders and Strengthen Community Capacity

Developing the regional infrastructure necessary to make Appalachia competitive requires a cadre of visionary leaders and effective organizations that are able to strategically mobilize communities toward their goals.

Selected Strategies:
- Build the organizational capacity required to meet increasing demands related to technology, environmental standards, and changing revenue sources.
- Provide training, consultation, and financial support for local leaders and organizations to build their capacity to address infrastructure challenges.

- Support partnerships and regional efforts among local and state governments, nonprofit agencies, and citizens engaged in infrastructure development.
- Encourage water and sewer infrastructure development through self-help projects that use the skills and commitment of local communities.
- Support strategic planning initiatives for local organizations and agencies to capitalize on economic development opportunities created by the Appalachian Development Highway System.

Strategic Objective 3.2: Build and Enhance Basic Infrastructure

Communities must have adequate water and wastewater treatment systems and decent, affordable housing to sustain businesses, generate jobs, protect public health, and ensure a basic standard of living for residents. Many Appalachian communities continue to lack this basic infrastructure, compromising the Region's ability to pursue basic development activities. Investing in basic infrastructure is an investment in the wellness, as well as the economic potential, of Appalachia.

Selected Strategies:
- Make strategic investments that leverage federal, state, private, and local capital for the construction or improvement of basic public infrastructure that supports economic development or addresses a public health concern.
- Encourage planning, design, coordination, and construction practices that improve the energy efficiency of infrastructure investments.
- Support continued efforts to maintain and expand the Region's stock of safe, affordable housing.

Strategic Objective 3.3: Increase Access to and Use of Telecommunications Technology

Communities across the Appalachian Region, especially those in rural or economically distressed areas, face serious challenges in taking advantage of new information, computing, and telecommunications technologies that have the potential to expand their economic development horizons. Changing regulations have resulted in access issues for rural communities and reluctance on the part of service providers to make capital investments in less-dense areas where it is more difficult to generate adequate returns on investments.

Selected Strategies:
- Make strategic investments in high-speed telecommunications infrastructure to increase local and regional connectivity and affordability.

- Encourage the use of telecommunications applications in education, health care, business, and government initiatives.
- Provide assistance for telecommunications development that coincides with other public infrastructure development.

Strategic Objective 3.4: Preserve and Enhance Environmental Assets

Cleaning up defunct industrial sites, promoting environmentally sensitive industries, and providing responsible stewardship and use of Appalachia's natural assets can play a vital part in putting the Region on an equal economic footing with the rest of the nation. This includes the reclamation of former industrial sites and mine-impacted lands for viable use.

Selected Strategies:

- Raise awareness of and leverage support for the reclamation and redevelopment of brownfields and mine-impacted communities.
- Encourage eco-industrial development that can responsibly take advantage of the Region's natural-resource assets.
- Support regional planning and economic development that promote good stewardship of the Region's natural resources.
- Promote efforts to protect and enhance the quality of surface and ground water.

Strategic Objective 3.5: Promote the Development of an Intermodal Transportation Network

In the twenty-first century, growth and prosperity depend on the ability to develop intermodal transportation systems with fast, efficient, and dependable access to worldwide suppliers and markets. Appalachian communities and businesses must continue to strengthen support for intermodal transportation strategies

designed to improve access to Appalachia's transportation network (including aviation, local transit systems, railway systems, and inland waterways) as well as to increase the responsiveness of that network to the needs of businesses, communities, and residents.

Selected Strategies:

- Encourage the planning and development of infrastructure that enhances economic development opportunities presented by intermodalism.
- Construct access roads that link economic development opportunities to the Appalachian Development Highway System corridors and other transportation networks.

General Goal 4:
*Build the Appalachian Development Highway System
to Reduce Appalachia's Isolation*

For Appalachia to compete economically with communities across the nation, it must have a safe and efficient transportation system connecting it to national transportation networks. Because of its difficult terrain, Appalachia was largely bypassed by the national interstate highway system, leaving the Region with a network of winding two-lane roads, which presented a major barrier to development. When ARC was established, Congress, recognizing the importance of overcoming the Region's geographic isolation, authorized the construction of an interstate-quality highway system in Appalachia. The Appalachian Development Highway System (ADHS) was created, and is being built, to enhance economic development opportunities in the Region by providing access to markets for goods, to jobs for workers, to health care for patients, and to education for students.

The strong partnership of ARC, the U.S. Department of Transportation, and state departments of transportation will continue to oversee the planning and construction of the Appalachian Development Highway System. ARC will work to identify and overcome barriers to the timely completion of the ADHS.

Strategic Objective 4.1: Develop Leaders and Strengthen Community Capacity

Long-term strategic planning by local and regional leadership is critical to taking full advantage of the economic and community-building opportunities presented by existing and planned ADHS corridors. New outreach and awareness efforts are needed to help communities fully integrate the ADHS into their economic development planning.

- Encourage local and multi-jurisdictional forums to strengthen communication, awareness, and mutual understanding in support of continued ADHS development.
- Support collaboration and coordination between transportation and economic development interests to strengthen access to domestic and international markets and to maximize economic and employment benefits to the Region.

Strategic Objective 4.2: Promote the Successful Development of the ADHS

Successful development of the ADHS is an essential step toward fostering economic growth and enabling Appalachia to become a significant contributor to the national economy. When completed, the system will connect the 13 states in the Region with nationwide and global economic opportunities.

Selected Strategies:

- Work with federal and state departments of transportation to identify and overcome barriers to the development of ADHS sections in the location-study phase.
- Assist federal and state departments of transportation in solving design problems and moving ADHS sections to the construction phase.
- Promote a development approach for the ADHS that preserves the cultural and natural resources of the Region while enhancing economic opportunity.

Strategic Objective 4.3: Improve Planning to Enhance Multi-Jurisdictional Coordination and Efficiency

Completing the ADHS in a timely manner will require close coordination of activities on those segments of the system that cross state lines.

Selected Strategies

- Promote improved coordination of technical information, funding disbursements, and construction scheduling to facilitate the construction of ADHS highway state-line crossings.
- Support opportunities to expand public-private coordination to increase the availability of capital investments and improve the transportation capacity of the Region.

Strategic Objective 4.4: Encourage Intermodal Coordination

Reliable, safe, and cost-efficient access to domestic and international markets is essential for Appalachia to successfully compete in the global economy of the twenty-first century. Coordinating the ADHS and Access Road programs with the Region's rail, waterway, and aviation modes can establish Appalachia as an important link in the global supply chain.

Selected Strategies:

- Develop the ADHS as the foundation for a coordinated and balanced intermodal transportation system that maximizes the Region's access to domestic and international markets.
- Encourage the development of key regional transportation corridors (highway, rail, and waterway) that link intermodal inland ports with key coastal ports to strengthen domestic and global access and enhance the competitiveness of Appalachian businesses.

Strategic Objective 4.5: Enhance the Energy Efficiency of the Transportation System

Energy-efficient transportation is critical to ensuring the competitiveness of existing businesses and attracting new enterprise and employment opportunities to the Region. Appalachia's transportation network must be planned and developed to ensure cost- and energy-efficient access in a future of increasing energy costs.

Selected Strategies:

- Encourage planning, design, coordination, and construction practices that improve overall energy efficiency in the movement of Appalachian travelers and cargo.
- Support the development and application of advanced transportation technologies that reduce energy consumption and help ensure the competitiveness of the Region's businesses.

Strategic Objective 4.6: Develop a Transportation System that Enhances and Preserves the Region's Environmental Quality

Planning and developing a twenty-first-century transportation network to ensure domestic and international access while actively supporting the Region's environmental health is essential to the future of Appalachia's businesses, communities, and people.

Selected Strategies:

- Encourage planning, coordination, and cooperation to achieve a reliable, safe, and cost-efficient transportation system that can both contribute to the Region's economic success and help protect its environmental quality.
- Promote the use of technologies that reduce the environmental impact of moving Appalachia's travelers and cargo.

Status of the Appalachian Development Highway System

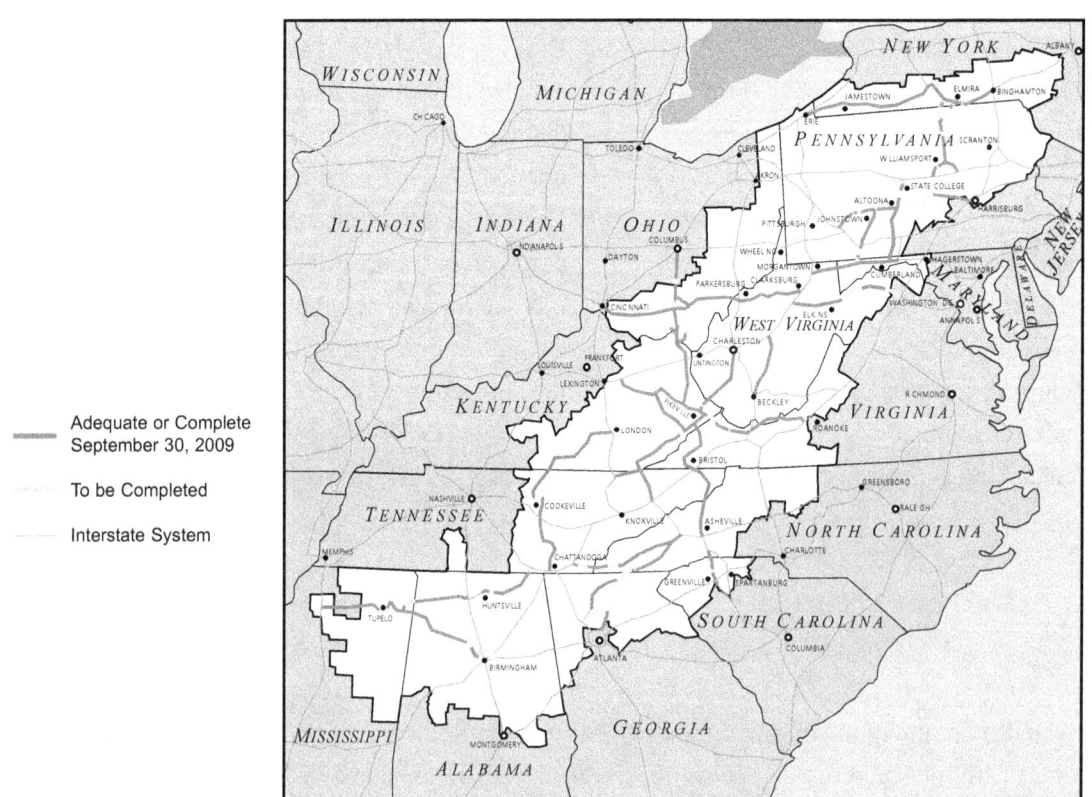

Adequate or Complete
September 30, 2009

To be Completed

Interstate System

Regional Priorities

In consultation with its partners, ARC may identify a limited number of strategic objectives annually as regional priorities. Regional priorities can reflect the need to redouble efforts in one or more goal areas to meet the Commission's six-year performance goals. The regional priority status can support and promote innovation in a particular goal area, or use ARC resources to focus on a sector of unique opportunity or underperformance.

Regional priorities support the strategic plan by coordinating a concerted effort by the 13 Appalachian states and federal government to address an area of critical importance. The designation of a strategic objective as a regional priority can involve the allocation of additional resources to that strategic objective. The targeted resources may be special advisory councils with the charge to develop region-wide activities; or regional priority status may involve the use of special funds earmarked for a specific strategic objective.

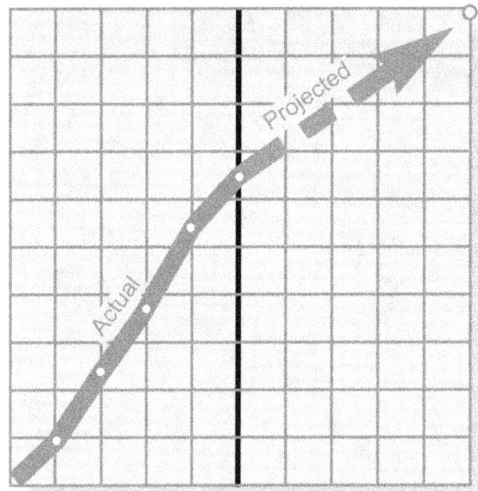

Performance Measures

As an investor in grassroots economic development, ARC's performance is in large measure dependent on the achievements of its local, state, and regional partners. To measure its effectiveness, ARC will look at the following four areas of performance:

- **Leverage.** ARC will measure additional public and private financial and technical support attracted by Commission investments.
- **Jobs.** ARC will gauge its involvement in job-generating programs by measuring both jobs created and jobs retained.
- **Employability.** ARC will measure improvements in high school graduation rates, increases in college attendance and graduation rates, the number of participants completing workforce training programs, and the number of children served in early childhood education programs.

- **Infrastructure Development and Connectivity.** ARC will look at the number of citizens served by new or improved infrastructure; connections made between modes of transportation, particularly between railways and highways; and highway miles opened to traffic.

Performance Goals

Assuming ARC's annual funding remains at the current level, the Commission is committed to the following six-year and twelve-year performance goals:

Six-Year Performance Goals

- 120,000 jobs will be created or retained.
- 120,000 households will be served with new or improved water and sewer infrastructure.
- 120,000 citizens of the Region will benefit from enhanced education and job-related skills.

- 150 miles of the Appalachian Development Highway System will be opened to traffic (based on the current level of transportation funding from the U.S. Congress).

Twelve-Year Performance Goals
- 240,000 jobs will be created or retained.
- 240,000 households will be served with new or improved water and sewer infrastructure.
- 240,000 citizens of the Region will benefit from enhanced education and job-related skills.
- 300 miles of the Appalachian Development Highway System will be opened to traffic (based on the current level of transportation funding from the U.S. Congress).

The Appalachian Regional Commission tracks the programs it supports and reports its findings regarding performance on a yearly basis. ARC's current performance and accountability report can be found on the ARC Web site at www.arc.gov.

Human Resources

ARC is composed of the governors of the 13 Appalachian states and a presidential appointee representing the federal government. The governors elect one of their members each year to serve as the states' co-chair; the federal representative serves as the federal co-chair.

Each year, the governors develop state Appalachian strategies, which are reviewed and approved at a meeting of all the governors and the federal co-chair.

After the strategies have been approved, the governors submit proposed projects to ARC, where they are reviewed by the Commission's program analysts. The process is completed when the federal co-chair reviews each project and formally approves it.

To meet its strategic objectives, the Appalachian Regional Commission relies on experienced, professional staff to deliver the following five critical skill sets:

- **Networking and Grassroots Empowerment.** Providing stakeholders with access to critical partners and essential organizational support.
- **Technical Expertise.** Guiding leaders in the Region through infrastructure and program development and delivery.
- **Leadership and Advocacy.** Representing the priorities of the Region to state and federal leaders.
- **Oversight, Management, and Quality Control.** Ensuring a high-quality result.
- **Communication.** External and internal communication of ARC plans, programs, and activities.

Federal and Commission staff are centrally located in Washington, D.C., to deliver services to the entire Region. State-funded staff are located in each of the 13 Appalachian states, with a regional representative located in Washington, D.C. Provision of staff by each of the states exhibits their commitment to the ARC partnership. This unique partnership serves to reduce the federal overhead expenses of operating the program while concentrating efforts on high-quality program management.

Program Management

ARC is committed to an administrative structure that encourages the highest-quality performance and supports the greatest amount of organizational flexibility. ARC manages programs and activities by providing staff focus in the following five areas:

- **Support to Local Development Districts.** ARC staff provide support and services to the local development districts, including information and technical assistance for planning and grant making, professional development training, and administration. See Appendix C for a directory of the local development districts.

- **Program Support.** ARC staff implement programs in partnership with federal and local organizations. Upon request, ARC staff provide technical assistance to partners on infrastructure, human resource development, and organizational capacity building.

- **Planning and Research.** ARC staff assist stakeholders by reviewing relevant state strategies, collecting data, and assisting with the creation of performance measures. ARC planners and researchers evaluate projects, manage the research portfolio for the Commission, and collect and analyze data to assess the effectiveness of the ARC strategic plan.

- **Outreach.** ARC staff provide communications support both internally and externally to stakeholders and strategic decision makers; support ARC-sponsored events and meetings; and create and support regional councils, working groups, and task forces that focus on specific regionwide challenges and opportunities.

- **Finance and Administration.** ARC staff perform all financial management, accounting, and budget-support functions for the organization; maintain the grants-management information system and other information technology operations; manage the ARC Web site, publications, and other administrative functions; and handle procurement and supply.

Communication

In order to ensure the implementation of the ARC strategic plan, the Commission will communicate the goals, objectives, and strategies of the plan throughout the agency and to the regional partners. Communication within the agency will involve an ongoing process of sharing the challenges and opportunities of moving the Region to national socioeconomic parity. ARC will communicate the new plan and strategies to the regional partners through newsletters, conferences, Commission meetings, the ARC Web site, and local development district workshops. This will be an ongoing process, with regular reporting at conferences and events.

ARC staff will be accountable for monitoring and communicating progress in achieving the mission, goals, and objectives.

Appendices

Appalachian Regional Commission
Strategic Plan

2011–2016

Strategic Planning Process Overview

ARC's six-month strategic planning process encompassed three phases: discovery, synthesis, and consensus. The process included extensive participation by Appalachian citizens, the ARC federal co-chair, the Appalachian governors' ARC alternates, representatives of the Region's 73 local development districts, and other key stakeholders, including congressional staff, members of local governments, community development corporations, and local business groups.

ARC's 2005–2010 strategic plan provided the foundation for the 2011–2016 strategic plan. The process for developing the new plan involved six steps: (1) holding field forums to obtain citizen input; (2) conducting research and consultations with experts on issues identified in the field forums, and conducting a socioeconomic review including an assessment of the Region's economy; (3) hosting a series of online town hall meetings to prioritize regional issues; (4) holding a synthesis session to review the findings of the online town hall meetings, field forums, and research in order to identify issues, opportunities, goals, and strategies for the strategic plan; (5) holding a consensus session to review the draft plan and make amendments as needed; and (6) adopting the new strategic plan.

The first step in the planning process involved obtaining citizen input on high-priority regional issues. ARC held five field forums—one each in Pennsylvania, North Carolina, Alabama, Kentucky, and West Virginia. More than 300 citizens participated in the forums, in addition to representatives from ten federal agencies, who participated both to support the ARC planning process and to prepare for a new multi-agency federal Appalachian Regional Development Initiative. Forty-two regional issues were identified in the forums, ranging from job-creation problems to natural-resource opportunities.

ARC then conducted research and consultations on regional issues and opportunities, after which the 42 issues identified in the field forums were presented to regional audiences through a series of online town hall meetings, in which par-

ticipants were invited to rank each issue. Twenty high-priority issues were identified through this process:

1. Growing jobs with local assets and local resources.
2. Assisting existing businesses in the Appalachian Region.
3. Developing regional solutions to problems.
4. Diversifying the local economic base.
5. Encouraging sustainable economic use of natural resources.
6. Investing in clinical care in areas without basic services.
7. Developing public/private partnerships.
8. Improving the college graduation rate in Appalachia.
9. Investing in broadband infrastructure.
10. Investing in long-term planning and strategic planning.
11. Conserving the natural places in Appalachia for eco-tourism.
12. Improving the job readiness of high school graduates.
13. Investing in high-tech worker training and retraining.
14. Preventing the pollution of surface water and ground water.
15. Investing in job readiness of community college graduates.
16. Promoting an entrepreneurial education at all levels of education.
17. Improving the energy efficiency of buildings.
18. Recruiting new industries to Appalachia.
19. Increasing the availability of capital.
20. Extending infrastructure to support job creation.

After the results of the field forums and online town hall meetings were analyzed, ARC held two working sessions with representatives of the 13 Appalachian states and the ARC federal staff to develop the elements of the new strategic plan, reflecting the current issues and concerns of the Region's citizens. The new strategic plan developed during these sessions was adopted by the Commission in November 2010. The plan gives a focus to ARC investments in jobs, infrastructure, education, and training while considering the need to conserve energy and protect the natural environment.

ARC STRATEGIC PLANNING PROCESS 2010

PHASE ONE:
DISCOVERY AND LISTENING

FIELD FORUMS	RESEARCH AND CONSULTATIONS	ONLINE TOWN HALL MEETINGS

North Field Forum

North Central Field Forum

South Central Field Forum

Southeast Field Forum

Southwest Field Forum

Identification of Regional Issues and Opportunities

Socioeconomic Review

Preparation of issues notebook with one-page summary of each critical issue

Issue Review

ARC Consultations on Program Issues and Opportunities

Research on Program Issues and Opportunities

Local Development Districts

Northern Appalachia

Central Appalachia

Southern Appalachia

FEBRUARY–MARCH 2010	APRIL 2010	MAY–JUNE 2010	JUNE–JULY 2010

MOVING APPALACHIA FORWARD

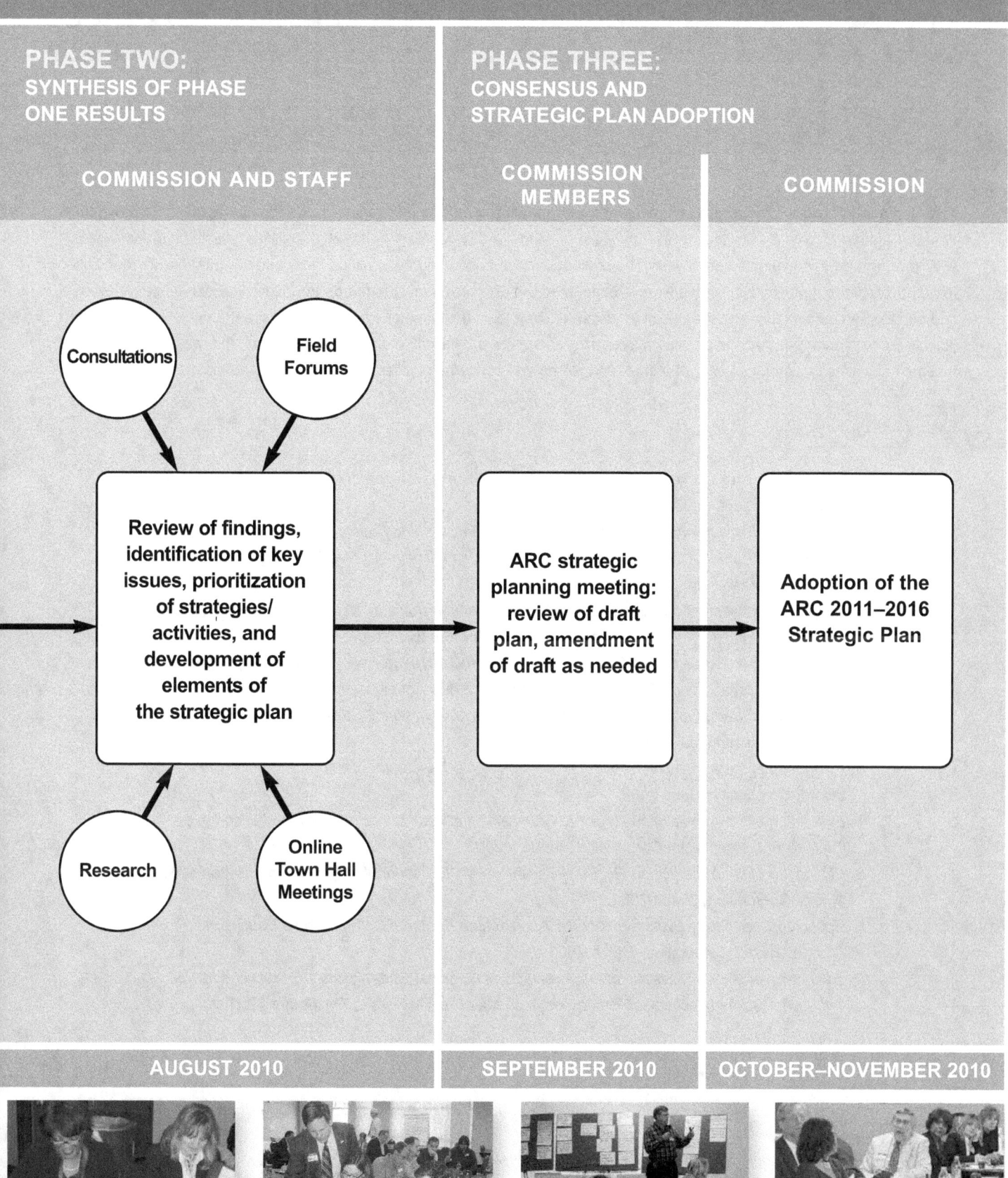

PHASE TWO:
SYNTHESIS OF PHASE
ONE RESULTS

COMMISSION AND STAFF

PHASE THREE:
CONSENSUS AND
STRATEGIC PLAN ADOPTION

COMMISSION
MEMBERS

COMMISSION

Consultations

Field
Forums

Review of findings,
identification of key
issues, prioritization
of strategies/
activities, and
development of
elements of
the strategic plan

Research

Online
Town Hall
Meetings

ARC strategic
planning meeting:
review of draft
plan, amendment
of draft as needed

Adoption of the
ARC 2011–2016
Strategic Plan

AUGUST 2010

SEPTEMBER 2010

OCTOBER–NOVEMBER 2010

Program Evaluations and Research Used in Preparing the Strategic Plan

ARC has a long history of using program evaluations to measure program effectiveness and identify areas for improvement. These evaluations, plus Commission research, were used in the development of the 2011–2016 strategic plan. A different ARC program area is evaluated each year. The evaluations are conducted by qualified independent, third-party organizations (e.g., private firms, universities) whose work is conducted under professional standards to ensure independence, relevance, and quality. Evaluations focus on the extent to which ARC projects have achieved, or contribute to the achievement of, their objectives. Particular emphasis is placed on assessing the utility and validity of the output and outcome measures. ARC's research activities focus on new program areas, problems and concerns of citizens, and the root causes of economic distress.

Evaluations

1. *Economic Impact Study of Completing the Appalachian Development Highway System*. Cambridge Systematics, June 2008.
2. *Creating an Entrepreneurial Appalachian Region: Findings and Lessons from an Evaluation of the Appalachian Regional Commission's Entrepreneurship Initiative 1997–2005*. RUPRI Center for Rural Entrepreneurship, April 2008.
3. *Program Evaluation of the Appalachian Regional Commission's Infrastructure and Public Works Projects*. BizMiner/Brandow Company, Inc., and EDR Group, October 2007.
4. *Evaluation of the Appalachian Regional Commission Oak Ridge National Laboratory Summer Institute for Math/Science/Technology*. Academy for Educational Development, March 2006.
5. *Evaluation of the Appalachian Regional Commission's Community Capacity–Building Projects*. Westat Corporation, July 2004.
6. *Evaluation of the Appalachian Regional Commission's Telecommunications Projects: 1994–2000*. Westat Corporation, June 2003.
7. *Evaluation of the Appalachian Regional Commission's Vocational Education and Workforce Training Projects*. Westat Corporation, January 2002.
8. *Evaluation of the Appalachian Regional Commission's Educational Projects: Final Report (Vol. 1)*. Westat Corporation, March 2001.
9. *Collected Case Study Evaluations of the Appalachian Regional Commission's Educational Projects (Vol. 2)*. Westat Corporation, March 2001.
10. *Evaluation of the Early Stages of the Appalachian Regional Commission's Entrepreneurship Initiative*. Regional Technology Strategies, Inc., March 2001; revised December 2001.

Research Reports

1. *Economic Impact of Rockslides in Tennessee and North Carolina*. HDR Decision Economics, Inc., May 2010.
2. *Industry Structure and Company Strategies of Major Domestic and Foreign Wind and Solar Energy Manufacturers: Opportunities for Supply Chain Development in Appalachia*. Pennsylvania State University, November 2009.

3. *Developing and Assessing Potential Forward-Looking Distress Indicators for the Appalachian Region*. Ohio State University, Mississippi State University, Pennsylvania State University, July 2009.

4. *Energy Efficiency in Appalachia: How Much More is Available, at What Cost, and by When?* Southeast Energy Efficiency Alliance, March 2009; revised May 2009.

5. *An Analysis of Mental Health and Substance Abuse Disparities & Access to Treatment Services in the Appalachian Region*. University of Chicago and East Tennessee State University, August 2008.

6. *An Assessment of Alternative Measures for Determining Economically Distressed Counties and Areas in the Appalachian Region*. Ohio State University, Mississippi State University, Pennsylvania State University, March 2008.

7. *Underlying Socioeconomic Factors Influencing Health Disparities in the Appalachian Region*. West Virginia University, March 2008.

8. *Sources of Regional Growth in Non-Metro Appalachia*. Economic Development Research Group, Inc., Regional Technology Strategies, Inc., Massachusetts Institute of Technology, Revised 2007.

9. *Energizing Appalachia: Global Challenges and the Prospect of a Renewable Future*. Pennsylvania State University, September 2007.

10. *Standards of Living in Appalachia: 1960–2000*. University of Chicago, Population Reference Bureau, University of Maryland, September 2007.

11. *The Upskilling of Appalachia: Earnings and the Improvement of Skill Levels, 1960–2000*. University of Chicago, Population Reference Bureau, University of Maryland, September 2007.

12. *Access to Capital and Credit for Small Businesses in Appalachia*. National Community Reinvestment Coalition, April 2007.

13. *Non-Renewable Energy Innovation: Research to Support the Appalachian Energy Initiative*. Global Insight, Inc., September 2006.

14. *National and State Energy Policy Trends*. The Keystone Center, August 2006.

15. *Creating an Energy Blueprint for Appalachia: Results of the ARC-ORCAS Energy Workshops*. Oak Ridge Center for Advanced Studies, August 2006.

16. *Energy Efficiency and Renewable Energy in Appalachia: Policy and Potential*. Marshall University CBER, July 2006.

17. *Economic Development Potential of Conventional and Potential Alternative Energy Sources in Appalachian Counties*. Pennsylvania State University, June 2006.

18. *Displacement in Appalachia and the Non-Appalachian United States, 1993–2003: Findings Based on Five Displaced Worker Surveys*. Keystone Research Center, December 2005.

19. *Drinking Water and Wastewater Infrastructure: An Analysis of Capital Funding and Funding Gaps*. University of North Carolina, July 2005.

20. *Assessing the Impact of Trade Liberalization on Import-Competing Industries in the Appalachian Region*. Dartmouth University, Yale University, July 2005.

21. *Changing Patterns of Poverty and Spatial Inequality in Appalachia*. Ohio State University, April 2005.

22. *Creating Regional Advantage in Appalachia: Towards a Strategic Response to Global Economic Restructuring*. Keystone Research Center, April 2005.

23. *Emerging Patterns of Population Redistribution and Migration in Appalachia.* Ohio State University, April 2005.

24. *Trends in National and Regional Economic Distress: 1960–2000.* Ohio University, April 2005.

25. *Population Growth and Distribution in Appalachia: New Realities.* Population Reference Bureau, January 2005.

26. *Underemployment in Appalachia and the Rest of the United States, 1996–2004.* Keystone Research Center, January 2005.

27. *Meeting the Transportation Challenges of the 21st Century: Intermodal Opportunities in the Appalachian Region.* Rahall Transportation Institute, Wilbur Smith Associates, December 2004.

28. *Meeting the Transportation Challenges of the 21st Century: Intermodal Case Studies.* Rahall Transportation Institute, Wilbur Smith Associates, December 2004.

29. *Meeting the Transportation Challenges of the 21st Century: Economic Benefits of Intermodal Efficiencies.* Rahall Transportation Institute, Wilbur Smith Associates, December 2004.

30. *Analysis of Global Competitiveness of Selected Industries and Clusters in the Appalachian Region.* Jack Faucett Associates, Economic Development Research Group, November 2004.

31. *An Analysis of Disparities in Health Status and Access to Health Care in the Appalachian Region.* West Virginia University, September 2004.

32. *Labor Market Performance, Poverty, and Income Inequality in Appalachia.* Syracuse University, University of Maryland, September 2004.

33. *A "New Diversity": Race and Ethnicity in the Appalachian Region.* Population Reference Bureau, September 2004.

34. *Educational Attainment in Appalachia.* Population Reference Bureau, May 2004.

35. *Households and Families in Appalachia.* Population Reference Bureau, May 2004.

36. *The Aging of Appalachia.* Population Reference Bureau, April 2004.

37. *Housing and Commuting Patterns in Appalachia.* Population Reference Bureau, January 2004.

38. *Appalachia at the Millennium: An Overview of Results from Census 2000.* Population Reference Bureau, June 2003.

39. *The Appalachian Economy, Establishment and Employment Dynamics, 1982–1997: Evidence from the Longitudinal Business Database.* Bureau of the Census Center for Economic Studies, May 2003.

40. *An Analysis of the Financial Conditions of Health Care Institutions in the Appalachian Region and their Economic Impacts.* Project HOPE, December 2002.

41. *Regional Technology Assets and Opportunities: The Geographic Clustering of High-Tech Industry, Science and Innovation in Appalachia.* University of North Carolina, August 2002.

42. *Links to the Future: The Role of Information and Telecommunications Technology in Appalachian Economic Development.* University of Texas, April 2002; updated June 2004.

43. *Comparing Electricity Deregulation in California and Pennsylvania: Implications for the Appalachian Region*. Center for Economic and Environmental Risk Assessment. Pennsylvania State University, January 2002.

44. *Analysis of Business Formation, Survival, and Attrition Rates of New and Existing Firms and Related Job Flows in Appalachia*. The Brandow Company, October 2001.

45. *An Assessment of Labor Force Participation Rates and Underemployment in Appalachia*. Keystone Research Center, August 2001.

46. *Manufacturing Wage Inequality in the Appalachian Region: 1963–1992*. University of Texas, May 2001.

47. *Handbook for Assessing Economic Opportunities from Appalachian Development Highways*. Economic Development Research Group and Cambridge Systematics, March 2001.

48. *A Study on the Current Economic Impacts of the Appalachian Coal Industry and its Future in the Region*. University of Kentucky, March 2001.

ARC Organizational Structure

The Partnership Model

The Appalachian Regional Commission has 14 members: the governors of the 13 Appalachian states and a federal co-chair, who is appointed by the president and confirmed by the Senate. Each year one governor is elected by his or her peers to serve as the states' co-chair. The partnership nature of ARC is evident in its policy making: the governors and the federal co-chair share responsibility for determining all policies and making spending decisions. The federal co-chair has one vote, and the 13 governors share one vote, on all Commission decisions. Accordingly, all program strategies, allocations, and other policy must be approved by both a majority of the governors and the federal co-chair. This consensus model ensures close collaboration between the federal and state partners in carrying out the mission of the agency. It also gives the Commission a character that distinguishes it from typical federal executive agencies and departments.

An alternate federal co-chair, who is also appointed by the president and confirmed by the Senate, has authority to act as the federal co-chair in his or her absence. Each governor appoints an alternate who oversees state ARC business and serves as the state-level point of contact for those seeking ARC assistance. Grassroots participation in implementing ARC programs is provided through local development districts, multi-county agencies with boards made up of elected officials, businesspeople, and other local leaders. (A list of local development districts in Appalachia begins on page 34.)

In all, there are only 11 federal positions in the Commission, including the federal co-chair's staff and the staff of the Office of Inspector General.

The Commission members appoint an executive director to serve as the chief executive, administrative, and fiscal officer. The executive director and staff are not federal employees. Fifty percent of the cost for the Commission's staff and other administrative activities is paid by the federal government; 50 percent is paid by the 13 Appalachian states. There are 48 Commission staff positions. Commission staff are charged with serving both the federal and the state members impartially in carrying out ARC programs and activities, and they provide the technical program management, planning and research, legal support, and financial/administrative management necessary to conduct these programs and activities.

Intergovernmental Cooperation

ARC's program authority encompasses a full range of federal domestic activities, including enterprise development, education and training, health care, export promotion, telecommunications, water and sewer infrastructure, and highway construction. Because of its limited appropriation, the Commission has always emphasized collaboration with public and private resources to accomplish its mission. ARC funding and technical assistance help communities leverage private and state funds, as well as other federal funds. ARC's highly flexible funds are often referred to as "glue money," which, although often a small part of projects, helps make them possible.

A special provision of the Appalachian Regional Development Act authorizes ARC to operate in part as a supplemental grant program. This authority allows ARC funds to be used to increase the allowable participation under federal grant programs, enabling grantees to participate in programs for which they would otherwise be ineligible. In addition, it involves appropriate federal entities to ensure not only program coordination but also compliance with all applicable laws, such as environmental and labor requirements. Accordingly, about half of past ARC grants have been administered under agreements with up to a dozen federal agencies, mainly the Economic Development Administration, USDA Rural Development, the Tennessee Valley Authority, the U.S. Department of Housing and Urban Development, and the Federal Highway Administration. Other agreements have involved such agencies as the Army Corps of Engineers and the U.S. Departments of Energy, Labor, and Health and Human Services.

ARC has also teamed with a range of national and regional foundations on special projects and initiatives over the years.

ARC Organization Chart

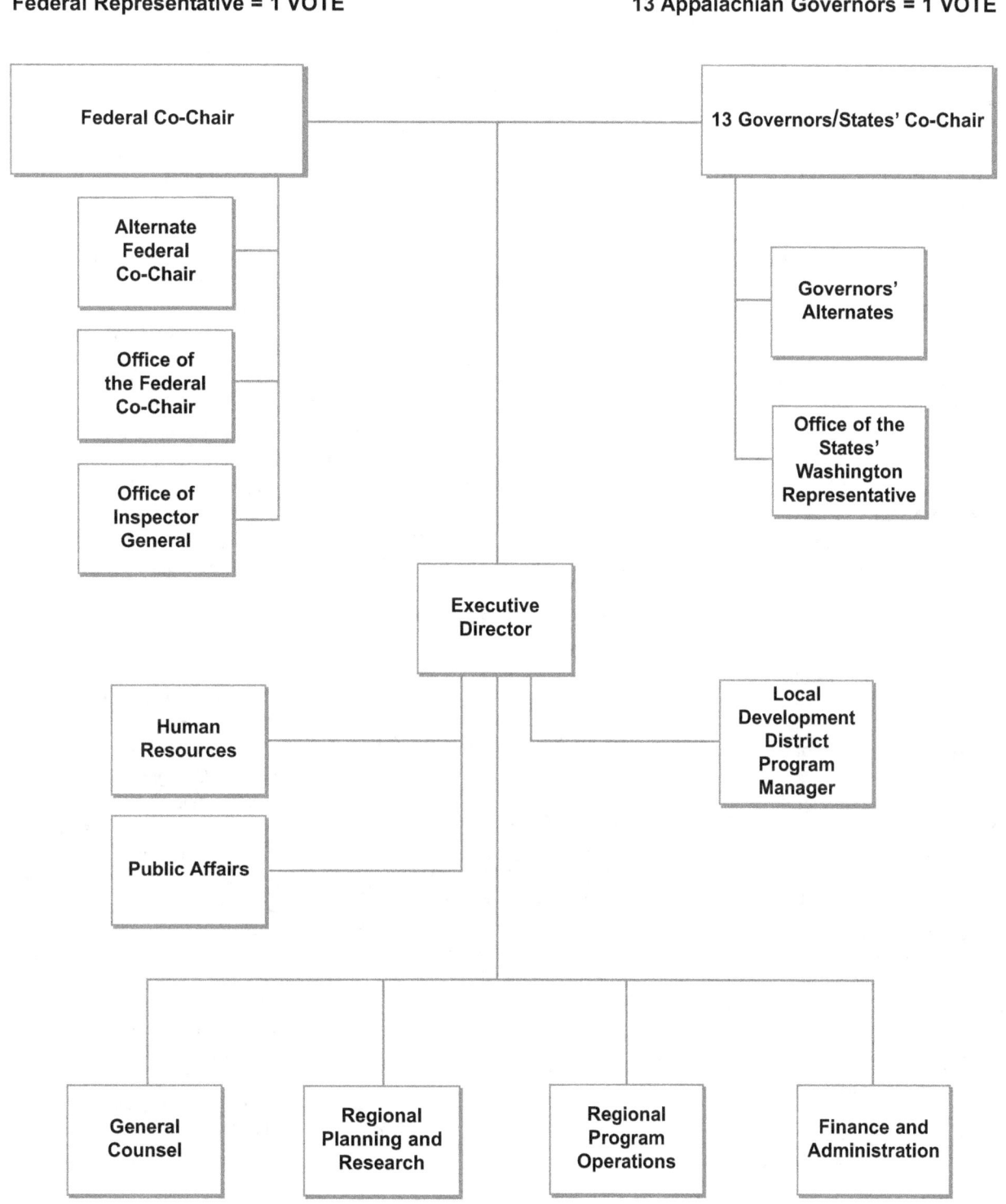

Federal Representative = 1 VOTE

13 Appalachian Governors = 1 VOTE

Federal Co-Chair

13 Governors/States' Co-Chair

Alternate Federal Co-Chair

Office of the Federal Co-Chair

Office of Inspector General

Governors' Alternates

Office of the States' Washington Representative

Executive Director

Local Development District Program Manager

Human Resources

Public Affairs

General Counsel

Regional Planning and Research

Regional Program Operations

Finance and Administration

Local Development Districts in the Appalachian Region

ALABAMA

1A/ Northwest Alabama Council of Local Governments
P.O. Box 2603
Muscle Shoals, Alabama 35662
256-389-0500
Web site: http://nacolg.com
Counties: Colbert, Franklin, Lauderdale, Marion, Winston

1B/ North Central Alabama Regional Council of Governments
216 Jackson Street, SE
Decatur, Alabama 35601
P.O. Box C
Decatur, AL 35602
256-355-4515
Web site: http://www.narcog.org
Counties: Cullman, Lawrence, Morgan

1C/ Top of Alabama Regional Council of Governments
5075 Research Drive, NW
Huntsville, Alabama 35805
256-830-0818
Web site: http://www.tarcog.org
Counties: DeKalb, Jackson, Limestone, Madison, Marshall

1D/ West Alabama Regional Commission
4200 Highway 69 North, Suite 1
P.O. Box 509
Northport, Alabama 35476-0509
205-333-2990
Web site: http://www.warc.info/
Counties: Bibb, Fayette, Hale, Lamar, Pickens, Tuscaloosa, (Greene)

1E/ Regional Planning Commission of Greater Birmingham
1731 First Avenue North, Suite 200
Birmingham, Alabama 35203
205-251-8139
Web site: http://www.rpcgb.org
Counties: Blount, Chilton, Jefferson, St. Clair, Shelby, Walker

1F/ East Alabama Regional Planning and Development Commission
1130 Quintard Ave., Suite 300
P.O. Box 2186
Anniston, Alabama 36202
256-237-6741
Web site: http://www.earpdc.org
Counties: Calhoun, Chambers, Cherokee, Clay, Cleburne, Coosa, Etowah, Randolph, Talladega, Tallapoosa

1H/ Central Alabama Regional Planning and Development Commission
430 South Court Street
Montgomery, Alabama 36104
334-262-4300
Web site: http://www.carpdc.com
Counties: Elmore, (Autauga, Montgomery)

1I/ South Central Alabama Development Commission
5900 Carmichael Place
Montgomery, Alabama 36117
334-244-6903
Web site: http://www.scadc.state.al.us
Counties: Macon, (Bullock, Butler, Crenshaw, Lowndes, Pike)

GEORGIA

2A/ Northwest Georgia Regional Commission
P.O. Box 1798
Rome, Georgia 30162-1798
706-295-6485
Web site: http://www.nwgrc.org
Counties: Bartow, Catoosa, Chattooga, Dade, Fannin, Floyd, Gilmer, Gordon, Haralson, Murray, Paulding, Pickens, Polk, Walker, Whitfield

2B/ Georgia Mountains Regional Commission
P.O. Box 1720
Gainesville, Georgia 30503
770-538-2626
Web site: www.gmrc.ga.gov
Counties: Banks, Dawson, Forsyth, Franklin, Habersham, Hall, Hart, Lumpkin, Rabun, Stephens, Towns, Union, White

2C/ Three Rivers Regional Commission
120 N. Hill Street
P. O. Box 818 (mailing address)
Griffin, Georgia 30224-0818
678-692-0510
Web site: http://www.threeriversrc.com
Counties: Carroll, Heard, (Butts, Coweta, Lamar, Meriwether, Pike, Spalding, Troup, Upson)

2D/ Atlanta Regional Commission
40 Courtland Street, NE
Atlanta, Georgia 30303
404-463-3100
Web site:
http://www.atlantaregional.com
Counties: Cherokee, Douglas, Gwinnett, (Clayton, Cobb, DeKalb, Fayette, Fulton, Henry, Rockdale)

2E/ Northeast Georgia Regional Commission
305 Research Drive
Athens, Georgia 30605-2795
706-369-5650
Web site: http://www.negrc.org
Counties: Barrow, Elbert, Jackson, Madison, (Clarke, Greene, Jasper, Morgan, Newton, Oconee, Oglethorpe, Walton)

KENTUCKY

3A/ Buffalo Trace Area Development District
P.O. Box 460
Maysville, Kentucky 41056
606-564-6894
Web site: http://www.btadd.com
Counties: Fleming, Lewis, Robertson, (Bracken, Mason)

3B/ FIVCO Area Development District
32 Fivco Court
Grayson, Kentucky 41143
606-929-1366
Web site: http://www.fivco.org
Counties: Boyd, Carter, Elliott, Greenup, Lawrence

3C/ Bluegrass Area Development District
699 Perimeter Drive
Lexington, Kentucky 40517
859-269-8021
Web site: http://www.bgadd.org
Counties: Clark, Estill, Garrard, Lincoln, Madison, Nicholas, Powell, (Anderson, Bourbon, Boyle, Fayette, Franklin, Harrison, Jessamine, Mercer, Scott, Woodford)

3D/ Gateway Area Development District
110 Lake Park Drive
Morehead, Kentucky 40351
606-780-0090
Web site: http://www.gwadd.org
Counties: Bath, Menifee, Montgomery, Morgan, Rowan

3E/ Big Sandy Area Development District
110 Resource Court
Prestonsburg, Kentucky 41653
606-886-2374
Web site: http://www.bigsandy.org
Counties: Floyd, Johnson, Magoffin, Martin, Pike

3F/ Lake Cumberland Area Development District, Inc.
P.O. Box 1570
Russell Springs, Kentucky 42642
270-866-4200
Web site: http://www.lcadd.org
Counties: Adair, Casey, Clinton, Cumberland, Green, McCreary, Pulaski, Russell, Wayne, (Taylor)

3H/ Cumberland Valley Area Development District
P.O. Box 1740
London, Kentucky 40743-1740
606-864-7391
Web site: http://www.cvadd.org
Counties: Bell, Clay, Harlan, Jackson, Knox, Laurel, Rockcastle, Whitley

3I/ Kentucky River Area Development District
917 Perry Park Road
Hazard, Kentucky 41701
606-436-3158
Web site: http://www.kradd.org
Counties: Breathitt, Knott, Lee, Leslie, Letcher, Owsley, Perry, Wolfe

3J/ Barren River Area Development District
177 Graham Avenue
Bowling Green, Kentucky 42101
270-781-2381
Web site: http://www.bradd.org
Counties: Edmonson, Hart, Metcalfe, Monroe, (Allen, Barren, Butler, Logan, Simpson, Warren)

MARYLAND

4A/ Tri-County Council for Western Maryland, Inc.
One Technology Drive, Suite 1000
Frostburg, Maryland 21532
301-689-1300
Web site: http://www.tccwmd.org
Counties: Allegany, Garrett, Washington

MISSISSIPPI

5A/ Northeast Mississippi Planning and Development District
P.O. Box 600
Booneville, Mississippi 38829
662-728-6248
Web site: http://www.nempdd.com
Counties: Alcorn, Benton, Marshall, Prentiss, Tippah, Tishomingo

5B/ Three Rivers Planning and Development District
P.O. Box 690
Pontotoc, Mississippi 38863
662-489-2415
Web site: http://www.trpdd.com
Counties: Calhoun, Chickasaw, Itawamba, Lee, Monroe, Pontotoc, Union, (Lafayette)

5C/ Golden Triangle Planning and Development District
P.O. Box 828
Starkville, Mississippi 39760-0828
662-324-7860
Web site: http://www.gtpdd.com
Counties: Choctaw, Clay, Lowndes, Noxubee, Oktibbeha, Webster, Winston

5D/ East Central Planning and Development District
P.O. Box 499
Newton, Mississippi 39345
601-683-2007
Counties: Kemper, (Clarke, Jasper, Lauderdale, Leake, Neshoba, Newton, Scott, Smith)

5E/ North Central Planning and Development District
711 South Applegate
Winona, Mississippi 38967
662-283-2675
Web site: http://www.ncpdd.org
Counties: Montgomery, Yalobusha, (Attala, Carroll, Grenada, Holmes, Leflore)

5F/ North Delta Planning and Development District
P.O. Box 1488
Batesville, Mississippi 38606-1488
662-561-4100
http://www.ndpdd.com
Counties: Panola, (Coahoma, DeSoto, Quitman, Tallahatchie, Tate, Tunica)

6A/ Southern Tier West Regional Planning and Development Board
Center for Regional Excellence
4039 Route 219, Suite 200
Salamanca, New York 14779
716-945-5301 Ext. 203
Web site:
http://www.southerntierwest.org
Counties: Allegany, Cattaraugus, Chautauqua

6B/ Southern Tier Central Regional Planning and Development Board
8 Denison Parkway East, Suite 310
Corning, New York 14830
607-962-5092
Web site: http://www.stcplanning.org/
Counties: Chemung, Schuyler, Steuben

6C/ Southern Tier East Regional Planning Development Board
375 State Street, Second Floor
Binghamton, New York 13901-2385
607-724-1327
Web site: http://www.steny.org/
Counties: Broome, Chenango, Cortland, Delaware, Otsego, Schoharie, Tioga, Tompkins

7A/ Southwestern Commission
125 Bonnie Lane
Sylva, North Carolina 28779
828-586-1962
Web site: http://www.regiona.org
Counties: Cherokee, Clay, Graham, Haywood, Jackson, Macon, Swain

7B/ Land-of-Sky Regional Council
339 New Leicester Hwy., Suite 140
Asheville, North Carolina 28806
828-251-6622
Web site: http://www.landofsky.org
Counties: Buncombe, Henderson, Madison, Transylvania

7C/ Isothermal Planning and Development Commission
P.O. Box 841
Rutherfordton, North Carolina 28139
828-287-2281
Web site: http://www.regionc.org
Counties: McDowell, Polk, Rutherford, (Cleveland)

7D/ High Country Council of Governments
486 New Market Blvd.
Boone, North Carolina 28607
828-265-5434
Web site: http://www.regiond.org
Counties: Alleghany, Ashe, Avery, Mitchell, Watauga, Wilkes, Yancey

7E/ Western Piedmont Council of Governments
P.O. Box 9026 (mailing address)
Hickory, North Carolina 28603
736 Fourth Street, SW
Hickory, North Carolina 28602
828-485-4230
Web site: http://www.wpcog.org
Counties: Alexander, Burke, Caldwell, (Catawba)

7I/ Northwest Piedmont Council of Governments
400 West Fourth Street, Suite 400
Winston-Salem, North Carolina 27101
336-761-2111
Web site: http://www.nwpcog.org
Counties: Davie, Forsyth, Stokes, Surry, Yadkin

8A/ Ohio Valley Regional Development Commission
9329 SR 220 East, Suite A
Waverly, Ohio 45690-9012
740-947-2853
Web site: http://www.ovrdc.org
Counties: Adams, Brown, Clermont, Gallia, Highland, Jackson, Lawrence, Pike, Ross, Scioto, Vinton, (Fayette)

8B/ Buckeye Hills–Hocking Valley Regional Development District
P.O. Box 520
Reno, Ohio 45773
740-374-9436
Web site: http://www.buckeyehills.org
Counties: Athens, Hocking, Meigs, Monroe, Morgan, Noble, Perry, Washington

8C/ Ohio Mid-Eastern Governments Association
P.O. Box 130
Cambridge, Ohio 43725-0130
740-439-4471
Web site:
http://www.omegadistrict.org
Counties: Belmont, Carroll, Columbiana, Coshocton, Guernsey, Harrison, Holmes, Jefferson, Muskingum, Tuscarawas

8D/ Eastgate Regional Council of Governments
City Centre One Building
100 East Federal Street, Suite 1000
Youngstown, Ohio 44503
330-779-3800
Web site: http://www.eastgatecog.org
Counties: Ashtabula, Mahoning, Trumbull

9A/ Northwest Pennsylvania Regional Planning and Development Commission
395 Seneca Street
P.O. Box 1127
Oil City, Pennsylvania 16301
814-677-4800
Web site:
http://www.nwcommission.org
Counties: Clarion, Crawford, Erie, Forest, Lawrence, Mercer, Venango, Warren

9B/ North Central Pennsylvania Regional Planning and Development Commission
651 Montmorenci Road
Ridgway, Pennsylvania 15853
814-773-3162
Web site: http://www.ncentral.com
Counties: Cameron, Clearfield, Elk, Jefferson, McKean, Potter

9C/ Northern Tier Regional Planning and Development Commission
312 Main Street
Towanda, Pennsylvania 18848
570-265-9103
Web site: http://www.northerntier.org
Counties: Bradford, Sullivan, Susquehanna, Tioga, Wyoming

9D/ Northeastern Pennsylvania Alliance
1151 Oak Street
Pittston, Pennsylvania 18640-3726
570-655-5581
Web site:
http://www.nepa-alliance.org
Counties: Carbon, Lackawanna, Luzerne, Monroe, Pike, Schuylkill, Wayne

9E/ Southwestern Pennsylvania Commission
425 Sixth Avenue, Suite 2500
Pittsburgh, Pennsylvania 15219-1852
412-391-5590
Web site: http://www.spcregion.org
Counties: Allegheny, Armstrong, Beaver, Butler, Fayette, Greene, Indiana, Washington, Westmoreland

9F/ Southern Alleghenies Planning and Development Commission
3 Sheraton Drive
Altoona, PA 16601
814-949-6513
Web site: http://www.sapdc.org
Counties: Bedford, Blair, Cambria, Fulton, Huntingdon, Somerset

9G/ SEDA–Council of Governments
201 Furnace Road
Lewisburg, Pennsylvania 17837
570-524-4491
Web site: http://www.seda-cog.org
Counties: Centre, Clinton, Columbia, Juniata, Lycoming, Mifflin, Montour, Northumberland, Perry, Snyder, Union

10A/ South Carolina Appalachian Council of Governments
P.O. Box 6668
Greenville, South Carolina 29606
864-242-9733
Web site: http://www.scacog.org
Counties: Anderson, Cherokee, Greenville, Oconee, Pickens, Spartanburg

11A/ Upper Cumberland Development District
1225 South Willow Avenue
Cookeville, Tennessee 38506-4194
931-432-4111
Web site: http://www.ucdd.org
Counties: Cannon, Clay, Cumberland, DeKalb, Fentress, Jackson, Macon, Overton, Pickett, Putnam, Smith, Van Buren, Warren, White

11B/ East Tennessee Development District
P.O. Box 249
Alcoa, Tennessee 37701-0249
865-273-6003
Web site:
http://www.discoveret.org/etdd
Counties: Anderson, Blount, Campbell, Claiborne, Cocke, Grainger, Hamblen, Jefferson, Knox, Loudon, Monroe, Morgan, Roane, Scott, Sevier, Union

11C/ First Tennessee Development District
3211 N. Roan Street
Johnson City, Tennessee 37601-1213
423-928-0224
Web site: http://ftdd.org/
Counties: Carter, Greene, Hancock, Hawkins, Johnson, Sullivan, Unicoi, Washington

11D/ South Central Tennessee Development District
P.O. Box 1346
Columbia, Tennessee 38402-1346
931-381-2040
Web site: http://www.sctdd.org
Counties: Coffee, Franklin, Lawrence, Lewis, (Bedford, Giles, Hickman, Lincoln, Marshall, Maury, Moore, Perry, Wayne)

11E/ Southeast Tennessee Development District
1000 Riverfront Parkway
P.O. Box 4757
Chattanooga, Tennessee 37402
423-266-5781
Web site: http://www.sedev.org
Counties: Bledsoe, Bradley, Grundy, Hamilton, Marion, McMinn, Meigs, Polk, Rhea, Sequatchie

12A/ LENOWISCO Planning District Commission
P.O. Box 366
Duffield, Virginia 24244
276-431-2206
Web site: http://www.lenowisco.org
Counties: Lee, Scott, Wise; and city of Norton

12B/ Cumberland Plateau Planning District Commission
P.O. Box 548
Lebanon, Virginia 24266
276-889-1778
Web site: http://cppdc.org
Counties: Buchanan, Dickenson, Russell, Tazewell

12C/ Mount Rogers Planning District Commission
1021 Terrace Drive
Marion, Virginia 24354
276-783-5103
Web site: http://www.mrpdc.org
Counties: Bland, Carroll, Grayson, Smyth, Washington, Wythe; and cities of Bristol and Galax

12D/ New River Valley Planning District Commission
6580 Valley Center Drive, Suite 124
Radford, Virginia 24141
540-639-9313
Web site: http://www.nrvpdc.org/
Counties: Floyd, Giles, Montgomery, Pulaski; and city of Radford

12E/ Roanoke Valley–Alleghany Regional Commission
P.O. Box 2569
Roanoke, Virginia 24010
540-343-4417
Web site: http://www.rvarc.org
Counties: Alleghany, Botetourt, Craig; and city of Covington, (Franklin, Roanoke; and cities of Roanoke and Salem)

12F/ Central Shenandoah Planning District Commission
112 MacTanly Place
Staunton, Virginia 24401
540-885-5174
Web site: http://www.cspdc.org
Counties: Bath, Highland, Rockbridge; and cities of Buena Vista and Lexington, (Augusta, Rockingham; and cities of Harrisonburg, Staunton, and Waynesboro)

12G/ West Piedmont Planning District Commission
1100 Madison Street
P.O. Box 5268
Martinsville, Virginia 24115-5268
276-638-3987
Web site: http://www.wppdc.org
Counties: Henry, Patrick, (Franklin, Pittsylvania)

13A/ Region I–Planning and Development Council
1439 E. Main Street, Suite 5
Princeton, West Virginia 24740
304-431-7225
Web site: http://www.regiononepdc.org
Counties: McDowell, Mercer, Monroe, Raleigh, Summers, Wyoming

13B/ Region 2–Planning and Development Council
P.O. Box 939 (mailing address)
Huntington, West Virginia 25712
740 Fourth Avenue
Huntington, West Virginia 25701
304-529-3357
Web site: http://www.region2pdc.org
Counties: Cabell, Lincoln, Logan, Mason, Mingo, Wayne

13C/ Region 3–B-C-K-P Regional Intergovernmental Council
315 D Street
South Charleston, West Virginia 25303
304-744-4258
Web site: http://www.wvregion3.org
Counties: Boone, Clay, Kanawha, Putnam

13D/ Region 4–Planning and Development Council
885 Broad Street, Suite 100
Summersville, West Virginia 26651
304-872-4970
Counties: Fayette, Greenbrier, Nicholas, Pocahontas, Webster

13E/ Region 5–Mid-Ohio Valley Regional Council
P.O. Box 247
Parkersburg, West Virginia 26102-0247
304-422-4993
Web site: http://www.movrc.org
Counties: Calhoun, Jackson, Pleasants, Ritchie, Roane, Tyler, Wirt, Wood

13F/ Region 6–Planning and Development Council
34 Mountain Park Drive
White Hall, West Virginia 26554
304-366-5693
Web site: http://www.regionvi.com
Counties: Doddridge, Harrison, Marion, Monongalia, Preston, Taylor

13G/ Region 7–Planning and Development Council
99 Edmiston Way, Suite 225
Buckhannon, West Virginia 26201
304-472-6564
Web site: http://www.regionvii.com
Counties: Barbour, Braxton, Gilmer, Lewis, Randolph, Tucker, Upshur

13H/ Region 8–Planning and Development Council
P.O. Box 849
Petersburg, West Virginia 26847
304-257-2448 or 304-257-1221
Web site: http://www.regioneight.org
Counties: Grant, Hampshire, Hardy, Mineral, Pendleton

13I/ Region 9–Eastern Panhandle Regional Planning and Development Council
400 W. Stephen Street, Suite 301
Martinsburg, West Virginia 25401
304-263-1743
Web site: http://www.region9wv.com
Counties: Berkeley, Jefferson, Morgan

13J/ Region 10–Bel-O-Mar Regional Council and Interstate Planning Commission
P.O. Box 2086
Wheeling, West Virginia 26003
304-242-1800
Web site: http://www.belomar.org
Counties: Marshall, Ohio, Wetzel; and Belmont County, Ohio

13K/ Region 11–Brooke-Hancock Regional Planning and Development Council
P.O. Box 82
Weirton, West Virginia 26062-0082
304-797-9666
Web site: http://www.bhjmpc.org
Counties: Brooke, Hancock

www.ingramcontent.com/pod-product-compliance
Lightning Source LLC
Chambersburg PA
CBHW081537280526
45788CB00010B/3263